John As

Eros Piano

Solo Piano Part

for Piano and Chamber Orchestra

Archive Edition

HENDON MUSIC

BOOSEY&HAWKES

AN IMAGEM COMPANY

DISTRIBUTED BY

HAL•LEONARD®
CORPORATION
7777 W. BLUEMOUND RD. P.O. BOX 13819 MILWAUKEE, WI 53213

www.boosey.com
www.halleonard.com

EROS PIANO

PIANO SOLO

JOHN ADAMS

Piano Solo

PIANO SOLO

EROS PIANO

SOLO PIANO

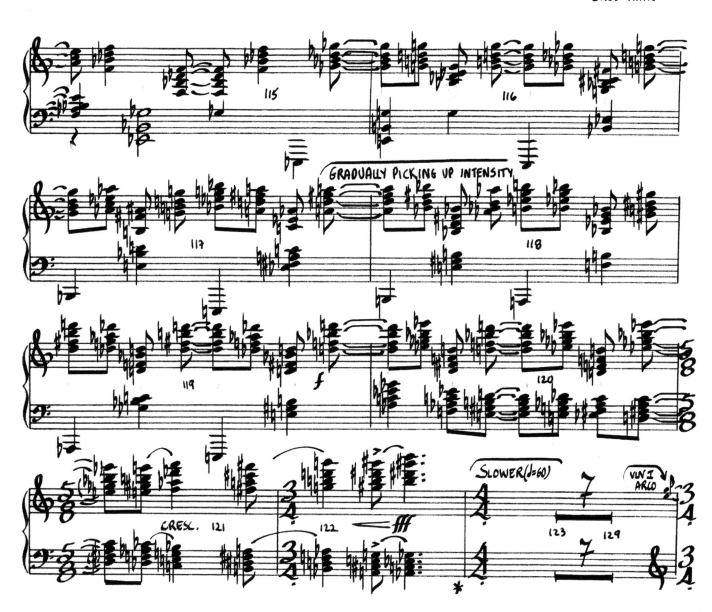

PIANO SOLO

PIANO SOLO

PIANO SOLO

EROS PIANO

DAVID OCKER, COPYIST

PIANO SOLO